52

CONVERSATIONS
TO HAVE WITH
YOUR TEEN

52

CONVERSATIONS TO HAVE WITH YOUR TEEN

DEREK T. ROWE

AMBASSADOR INTERNATIONAL
GREENVILLE, SOUTH CAROLINA & BELFAST, NORTHERN IRELAND

www.ambassador-international.com

52 Conversations to Have with Your Teen

ISBN: 978-1-62020-829-8
eISBN: 978-1-62020-835-9

Cover Design & Typesetting by Hannah Nichols
Ebook Conversion by Anna Riebe Raats
Author Photo by Teresa Jenkins

AMBASSADOR INTERNATIONAL
Emerald House
411 University Ridge, Suite B14
Greenville, SC 29601, USA
www.ambassador-international.com

AMBASSADOR BOOKS
The Mount
2 Woodstock Link
Belfast, BT6 8DD, Northern Ireland, UK
www.ambassadormedia.co.uk

The colophon is a trademark of Ambassador, a Christian publishing company.

To Jesus

To my wife Gabby, for your encouragement and love

To parents, for raising kids in the ways of the Lord

TABLE OF CONTENTS

HOW TO USE THIS BOOK

PURPOSE

This book is a platform from which you can make a big splash. It is meant to provoke and inspire. It is meant for thought and contemplation. Most of all, it is meant to provide you with a yearly plan for engaging in intentional conversations with your teenager. Many people are so busy running from event to event that intentional, deep conversations are often forgotten. This book will help you deepen your relationship with your teen with one important conversation each week of the year.

STRUCTURE

You will find four questions for each month of the year. You will also find an "Extra Weeks" question section with four more questions, bringing the total number of questions to fifty-two. You can use the miscellaneous questions for any month in which there is a fifth Sunday. Below each question, you will find two short paragraphs relating to each question. The first paragraph contains some general thoughts about the topic. The second paragraph contains a Bible verse that relates to the topic. You can use these two paragraphs to aid in preparing your thoughts for the conversation to come. After each set of paragraphs is a notes section. The notes section is for you to write down a few notes about the conversation, such as your teen's initial reaction and your thoughts about the conversation. You can use the notes section to write down whatever you think will be helpful when you revisit the question in the future.

YOUR TASK

Your task as the parent or adult is to ask your teen one question per week. The listed question is only your starting point for engaging in conversation. Ask the question (in your own words and voice), and wait for a response from your teen. As the conversation progresses, you will want to affirm your teen for responding, as well as ask some follow-up questions such as:

- "What makes you think that?"
- "Why do you believe that?"
- "Can you tell me more about that?"
- "What is an example of that?"

All of these questions and others will help you carry the conversation beyond a simple yes, no, or other one-phrase response. Follow-up questions are essential to successful conversation.

Where and when you begin these conversations will likely play a significant part of how well they go. For example, if your teen just lost her basketball game, it is probably not the best time to ask a question about the true meaning of Easter. Incorporate the questions into the normal parts of everyday life. You may ask the question at the dinner table, while you are making cookies, while you are playing a game together, or during a car ride. You know your teen the best to determine the best time and place each week to ask these questions.

After the conversation, jot down a few notes about your teen's response in the notes area provided after each question's section. The notes section is there so that you can recall your teen's answers to questions and your thoughts about the conversation. If you want to return to a specific topic at a later point in time, you will have a few notes to jog your memory.

ENCOURAGEMENT

I hope this book encourages you to meet a reasonable goal of connecting with your teen once a week this year. The teenage years are full of changes in mind, body, and thought. Teens are searching for their true friends. They want to fit in. They want to be accepted. They want to be known. They are starting to decide for themselves if God is actually real or if church is just a part of social life.

You are the greatest influence in your teen's life. You can be the one to show your teen love, to make him feel known, and to guide him in forming more of his own thoughts. If you are a Christian parent, you can and should be the main one to show your teen Who God is from Scripture and from the example you give him. Proverbs 29:15 says, "A rod of correction imparts wisdom, but a youth left to himself is a disgrace to his mother." Proverbs 22:6 says, "Teach a youth about the way he should go; even when he is old he will not depart from it."

Many youth today are simply left to their own devices to form their thoughts and navigate the world. I encourage you to use your God-given influence and position to raise godly sons and daughters. Part of the way you can do this is by building a relationship with your teen by finding out about his mind and heart and training him in godliness. This book will help you to do just that.

Are you ready to know and influence your teen better this year?

Ready?

Set?

Pray.

JANUARY

1.   WHAT WOULD YOU LIKE TO IMPROVE ABOUT YOURSELF THIS
YEAR?

The new year is a natural time to evaluate what goals you'd like to set for the year. As you also know, New Year's resolutions are often made and usually broken. Some say it is not even worth it to create goals because they probably won't be achieved anyway. Regardless of your outlook on resolutions, the new year is a great time to reconnect with your teen. It sneaks up on us the week after Christmas, while the kids are still on break from school. You can start the year off by asking your teen what goal he would like to set. What is going through his mind? Does he even think about setting an improvement goal for himself?

Renewal and improvement is something that God commands and expects from His people. Romans 12:2 (HCSB) says, "Do not be conformed to this age, but be transformed by the renewing of your mind, so that you may discern what is the good, pleasing, and perfect will of God." We are to always be in the process of becoming more like Jesus. Teens need their parents to model improvement and help them improve through the power of the Holy Spirit. Take a few moments and ask your teen how he would like to become better this year. You may be surprised at the answer.

NOTES:

_____

_____

_____

_____

_____

_____

_____

2. DO YOU THINK THAT GOD IS REAL?

On the surface, this may seem like a deep question—because it is. The question of the reality of God may be one that your sixth, seventh, or eighth grader may have never have had a conversation about. If you or your children have grown up going to church, it is safely assumed that God is real. However, have you ever thought about why? What makes you believe God is real? Maybe a circumstance, a certain relationship, or some other happening has helped you discover the reality of God. What about for your teen?

One way to know that God is real is by looking at creation. The stars, sun, moon, and earth all point to God as the Creator and Sustainer of all things. How did the sun begin to shine? How did the earth begin to rotate? How did trees grow? How did the ocean separate from the land? How did the stars get put into place? Genesis 1:1 says, "In the beginning God created the heavens and the earth." There are many ways to know God is real; one of those ways is by His creation. What does your teen think?

NOTES:

_____

_____

_____

_____

_____

_____

_____

3. What do you think about racism?

Racism is a subject that is handled very differently based on individual situations. Some families talk about racism a lot, while others seldom raise the issue. Some students are exposed to blatant racism every day, while some have not experienced racism firsthand. Either way, any turning on of the TV will expose racism in some way from TV shows to the news. Racism is still tackled, even if only briefly, in school curriculum—from slavery in the United States to the Civil Rights Movement to Black Lives Matter. The topic of race is one that every person should be informed of because it is in the current fabric of U.S. society.

What does the Bible say about racism? Acts 17:26 says, "From one man He has made every nationality to live over the whole earth and has determined their appointed times and the boundaries of where they live." God is the Creator of mankind. He first created Adam and Eve, and every nationality came about through them. With different skin colors, hair colors, eye colors, accents, and experiences, every single person is valuable to God. People may be culturally different, and that is great. God created man that way. However, every person is equally valuable in the sight of God. What are your teen's experiences or thoughts about racism?

NOTES:

_____

_____

_____

_____

_____

_____

_____

4.   DO YOU THINK THAT GOD IS GOOD?

Is God good? Is He good only sometimes or all the time? I think all people who believe in God want to say, "God is good, all the time; and all the time, God is good." It is easy to believe that God is good when your teen gets an "A" on her test or when she makes the basketball team. It is easy to praise God's goodness when everyone is healthy, and all the bills are paid. What about when things are not going so well? When someone is in the hospital? When we did not get the grade we thought we should? When the circumstances don't go the way we planned? Is God still good?

Psalm 119:68 says, "You are good, and You do what is good; teach me Your statutes." This Psalm says two important things about God:

- **God is good.** He is good in His character and in His nature. It is more than just having an attribute of goodness; He *is* goodness. If you know God, then you know what good is.

- **God does what is good.** Not only is God good, but His actions are good as well. He does good for His people. Everything He does to, through, and for us is ultimately for our good in some way. God never promises that life will be problem-free for Christians. In fact, in John 16:33 Jesus says that we will have trouble. However, God has overcome the world! In the troubles—Immanuel—"God is with us." God is still good, even when the current circumstances may not seem like it. Does your teen think God is good?

NOTES:

_____

_____

_____

_____

_____

_____

FEBRUARY

5. Have you been bullied this year?

The topic of bullying could be a sensitive one for your teen. It may even be a sensitive one for you. Most people have probably been bullied in some way at some point in their life. Some people are able to let bullying roll off their backs and some internalize it and hold on to it for years. Bullying is not okay in any way. Chances are, your teen has either been bullied, bullied someone else, or seen bullying in action. Unless you happen to have a close, verbal relationship with your teen, you may not know about these situations that occur when they are apart from you.

Matthew 5:44 says, "But I tell you, love your enemies and pray for those who persecute you." Jesus commands us not to get revenge on those who mistreat us. Instead, we are to pray for them. God has given the Christian the Holy Spirit and the power to walk in the light, even in a bullying circumstance. Being a light in the moment may not take away the pain of being bullied, but it will honor God because you are following His commands. Ask your teen about being bullied. It may be a great way to connect about something very personal to him.

NOTES:

_____

_____

_____

_____

_____

_____

_____

6. DOES GOD SHOW YOU THAT HE LOVES YOU?

If you are like most people, grasping God's love is difficult. We cannot physically see God, and most have never audibly heard God. However, we know that God loves us.

This may be a good question for you to answer for yourself as well. How does God show you that you are loved? Was it through a circumstance or another person? Was it something you read in Scripture? Are there certain ways God has provided for you?

Asking your teen this question will probably give her something to think about. Romans 5:8 says, "But God proves His own love for us in that while we were still sinners, Christ died for us!" One of the most significant ways that God shows His love for us is that He died for us. The Father sent Jesus into the sin-ridden world to be the sacrifice for sin. Jesus was beaten, killed on the cross, buried, and raised to life so that people could have an eternal relationship with Him. How your teen sees or does not see God's love will highly influence how your teen sees herself and the world.

NOTES:

_____

_____

_____

_____

_____

_____

_____

7. What season do you enjoy the most?

Seasons are interesting things that God has worked into the fabric of life. Some places feel as though there is only one season: summer or winter. Some places in the world function with a very distinct four-season model. Everyone experiences seasons in different ways, and each person has his favorite. Some like fall because the leaves change colors. Some like summer because they can play in water and wear shorts every day. Others like spring because of the blooming of many flowers. While yet more enjoy the snow and glisten of winter. Which is your favorite?

Scripture teaches that God is the One Who established the seasons. Psalm 74:17 says, "You set all the boundaries of the earth; You made summer and winter." God created the different seasons in different parts of the earth for various reasons. In many places, seasons signal the sowing and reaping times for the harvest. Each season has its unique features that make it enjoyable to humanity. What season is your teen's favorite? What characteristics make that particular season a top choice?

NOTES:

_____

_____

_____

_____

_____

_____

8. DO YOU KNOW WHAT THE GOSPEL IS?

What is the Gospel? How do you explain it in simple terms to someone else? The Gospel is the core of Christianity. The Gospel is the news that draws people into a relationship with God. "Gospel," translated from Greek, means "good news." The Gospel is the good news that is the heartbeat of the Christian faith. It is clear that many teens are not able to accurately describe the Gospel to someone else because they have not had to practice knowing the Gospel themselves or articulating it to someone else. In order to share the life-giving message of Christ to another person, the Gospel must be clearly understood.

1 Corinthians 15:3-4 says, "For I passed on to you as most important what I also received: that Christ died for our sins according to the Scriptures, that He was buried, that He was raised on the third day according to the Scriptures." This passage from 1 Corinthians states the main points of the Gospel, the good news of Jesus Christ.

John 3:16 is a complementary verse that says, "For God loved the world in this way: He gave His One and Only Son, so that everyone who believes in Him will not perish but have eternal life." God came to earth in the form of Jesus, died, was buried, and was raised again so that anyone who puts their faith in Him could have eternal life. Those are the simple, yet profound tenants of the Gospel. Does your teen understand, and can he articulate the Gospel?

NOTES:

_____

_____

_____

_____

_____

_____

_____

MARCH

9. What are you most afraid of?

This question could go a myriad of ways. The answer might be the boogey-man, though not likely at this stage in the game. It could be the fear of not being liked, being rejected, not being loved by Mom and Dad, not making the basketball team, or being afraid of heights. Fear is something that everyone has at some point in their lives. Some fears dissipate with time, and some fears stay for life. Fears can change as well, depending on what life events have happened.

What does the Bible say about fear? There are hundreds of passages about fear in Scripture. Psalm 27:1 says, "The Lord is my light and my salvation—whom should I fear? The Lord is the stronghold of my life—of whom should I be afraid?" God is the One Who illuminates our future. God is the One Who is the Cornerstone, the Stronghold of life. If we have trusted Him as our Savior, we can rest assured that we will ultimately spend forever with Him. While we will have troubles in this life, He will comfort us and see us through those trials. He wants good for us and wants us to go to Him to find comfort. What is a fear your teen has that can be shared and then turned over to God?

NOTES:

_____

_____

_____

_____

_____

_____

_____

10. DO YOU THINK READING THE BIBLE IS IMPORTANT?

If your teen has grown up in church for any length of time, she will know that the answer is yes. In preparation for asking this one, you may want to discover your answer to the question first. Do you think reading the Bible is important? If so, why do think it is important? Is it simply something to check off of the to-do list? Do you enjoy the time you get to spend in the Word? What benefits have you seen in your life from being in the Word regularly?

2 Timothy 3:16-17 says, "All Scripture is inspired by God and is profitable for teaching, for rebuking, for correcting, for training in righteousness, so that the man of God may be complete, equipped for every good work." God's Word, the Bible, is our main source for knowing God more. It is our supply for understanding our position in this life and finding out what God wants us to do and how God wants us to live. It is also the source for training up children in the Lord. The Bible is our primary source for growing in our relationship with Christ and allowing God to enable us to do good works. If we want to live lives that are honoring to Christ, we must be in the Word regularly. The key issue to explore is why your teen thinks reading the Bible is important. What personal stories can she share about being in the Word? This will probably be an opportunity to share how your time with God has impacted you in your everyday life.

NOTES:

_____

_____

_____

_____

_____

_____

_____

11.   What is one of the happiest times of your life?

Everyone loves happy times. Happiness is one of the things that all of humanity searches for in life. People find and experience happiness in different ways. When you are a little child, maybe playing in a sandbox makes you the happiest. When you are a grandparent, maybe watching a granddaughter be born makes you the happiest. For a teen, the happiest time may be a vacation, getting a good grade on a test, or getting something really cool for Christmas. Everyone has something that has made them happy at some point. If your teen comes up empty in response, you may have to jog his memory a little bit.

When are people the happiest? Psalm 144:15 says, "Happy are the people with such blessings. Happy are the people whose God is Yahweh." When all of our needs are met, when we turn to God as the Lord of life, then are we the happiest. It is comforting to know that God has our best interest in mind. As the psalmist says, when people acknowledge their God as Yahweh, they are happiest. Sometimes, receiving things, seeing something cool, or having an uplifting relationship with someone brings us happiness—and all of those things do, at times. However, that happiness is amplified when we realize that God is the Giver of all of those good things, and we can worship Him because of it. What things makes your teen happy? How can those things or experiences be traced back to God?

NOTES:

_____

_____

_____

_____

_____

_____

_____

12. WHY DO YOU THINK PEOPLE CELEBRATE EASTER?

Many people know about Easter—both Christians and non-Christians. Many people even go to some type of church service on Easter, even if they are not Christian. The Easter celebrations are usually full of fun things for kids—from the Easter Bunny to going on Easter egg hunts. People gather with their families to eat some ham, turkey, or barbeque. It can be very easy for the meaning and significance of Easter to get lost in all of the bright-colored shirts and dresses, fun activities, and, even, a church service. Here is an opportunity to take a few moments and reflect on the reason for celebrating Easter.

Luke 24:6-7 says, "He is not here, but He has been resurrected! Remember how He spoke to you when He was still in Galilee, saying, 'The Son of Man must be betrayed into the hands of sinful men, be crucified, and rise on the third day'?" Easter is about the resurrection of Jesus from the dead. Three days earlier, He was crucified on a Roman cross. On what we call Easter morning, the tomb was found to be empty because God raised Christ to life. The resurrection is one of the most important facets of Christianity because it shows that God even has the power over death. What is your teen's take on why we celebrate Easter?

NOTES:

_____

_____

_____

_____

_____

_____

_____

APRIL

13. WHO ARE SOME OF YOUR BEST FRIENDS IN SCHOOL?

Good friends are hard to come by. Friends are one of the biggest influences on teens growing up and going to school. Teens spend a lot of time with friends and want to fit in with them. Some kids even hang out with certain people in hopes of becoming good friends one day. There are also teens who have resorted to not making friends because they have had a bad interaction with other teens. Friends can be the ones who are the most encouraging or the most destructive. The importance of good friends cannot be overstated.

Proverbs 13:20 says, "The one who walks with the wise will become wise, but a companion of fools will suffer harm." In general, teens who have friends seeking to do the right thing will themselves do the right thing. Teens who have friends who are doing the wrong things will probably end up doing the wrong things. There can oftentimes be a conflict of interest when the desire to do right collides with the desire to fit in with a group. This is a tension many teens face. Who are the people your teen considers to be good friends? Why are they considered friends?

NOTES:

_____

_____

_____

_____

_____

_____

14. How do you think the world began?

This is a question every person is sure to ask at some point. With evolution being preached in schools and other worldviews preached elsewhere, where did everything begin? Was the world and everything we know created out of nothing? Was there a "big bang" that was initiated with no initiator? Did the world just happen to form by accident? All of these are valid questions and deserve exploration. Your teen is probably already navigating the options.

John 1:3 says, "All things were created through Him, and apart from Him not one thing was created that has been created." The truth is that we are not entirely sure how the world began or what that process looked like. We do know that God is the Creator of everything. He spoke, and things came into being. Unfortunately, no one was there with a video camera to record the beginning of everything. The important thing is that God is and was the Initiator of everything that exists, everything that we know. How does your teen think the world began?

NOTES:

_____

_____

_____

_____

_____

_____

_____

15. IF YOU COULD HAVE A SUPERPOWER, WHAT WOULD IT BE?

This should be a fun question for the week. Think about what your su-perpower would be. Would you want super strength like the Hulk? Or would you like to be able to swing from webs like Spider-Man? Would you want to be super-fast like The Flash? The superpower you choose is probably one that is extraordinary, one that would not actually be possible in real life. That is the fun of imagining. Take this week to explore the seemingly impossible and see what you would use a power for. Would you use it to help people, yourself, or both?

Aren't you interested to see where Scripture talks about superpowers? You didn't know there was one, did you? Mark 4:39 says, "He got up, rebuked the wind, and said to the sea, 'Silence! Be still!' The wind ceased, and there was a great calm." While this may not be a superpower as we normally think of it, this is greater than what we can come up with. Jesus Himself, God of the universe, is able to do what seems impossible to us. The waves were roaring, and the disciples were very afraid of the storm. They woke Jesus. Jesus spoke. The sea calmed. Just like that. God is greater than any superhero. What is your teen's favorite superpower?

NOTES:

_____

_____

_____

_____

_____

_____

_____

16. DO YOU THINK GOD IS FAIR?

Is God fair? Maybe we should define *fair* first. One definition, according to *Merriam-Webster's Dictionary*, is "marked by impartiality and honesty: free from self-interest, prejudice, or favoritism.[1]" While we all often want things to be fair, we know that the world is not fair. Sometimes, people do not get what they deserve; and other times, people get something that was unearned. There are some situations in which we wish that everything was fair, like getting a raise or getting the same number of Christmas presents for all the kids. There are other times that we are glad things are not so fair. Fairness could also mean "just." Typically, when we use the term *fair*, we use it to mean that a person's action should cause a specific outcome.

Based on the most commonly used meaning of the word, God is most definitely not fair. And that should be a relief to us all. Romans 6:23 says, "For the wages of sin is death, but the gift of God is eternal life in Christ Jesus our Lord." Since everyone has sinned, everyone deserves to spend eternity apart from God. However, in God's grace, He decides to give a special gift to those who put their trust in Him—the gift of eternal life. This is an instance where God is not fair, and the outcome benefits us! Does your teen think God is or should be fair?

NOTES:

_____

_____

_____

_____

_____

_____

_____

1 *Merriam-Webster*, s.v. "fair," December 12, 2016, https://www.merriam-webster.com.

MAY

17. What do you think about alcohol?

Should you have a conversation about alcohol consumption with your teen? Yes. Chances are they have already had this conversation with someone else if they have not had it with you. Alcohol is one of the topics that even people within the Christian community have differing opinions on. Some go as far as to say that all alcohol is sinful. Some say you should be able to consume whatever you please. The biblical stance is probably somewhere in between.

Ephesians 5:18 says, "And don't get drunk with wine, which leads to reckless actions, but be filled by the Spirit." Paul commands the church to not get drunk with alcohol. That seems to be the consistent stance throughout Scripture—not that the alcohol in itself is evil, but the effects from consuming too much are not glorifying to God. With that said, each family has their own convictions and rules for their house. There are also laws of the land to abide by. Has your teen been offered alcohol before? Is it talked about in school? What is her view on alcohol?

NOTES:

_____

_____

_____

_____

_____

_____

_____

18. Do you have a favorite Bible verse?

What is your favorite Bible verse? John 3:16 is a favorite verse for many people. It is probably because it is so central to the core message of the Bible. It could also be because it is one of the most advertised and published verses of the Bible. Oftentimes, favorite verses become favorites because they were utilized at a time when you needed God's Word for a particular situation. We remember these verses and commit them to memory. Verses are difficult to forget once we have them memorized.

Memorizing Scripture helps us in our daily walk with the Lord. Psalm 119:11 says, "I have treasured Your word in my heart so that I may not sin against You." When we treasure God's Word, it helps us focus on Jesus. We can then use the Word of God in trying situations to help keep us from sinning against Him. In today's age, we tend not to memorize as much because we can retrieve what we need online at the push of a button. However, spiritual vitality is greatly improved when we do memorize God's Word and do not rely only on the internet to find passages for us. What is your teen's favorite verse?

NOTES:

_____

_____

_____

_____

_____

_____

_____

19. WHAT DO YOU THINK ABOUT YOUR MOM?

Moms are one of God's greatest gifts. They work, cook, clean, and change diapers, amongst a myriad of other tasks. They are faithful and nurturing. They take care of you when you are sick. They are some of the most loving and caring people on the planet. If there is a child born, he came from a mom. Everyone's situation is different. Some kids live with their mom or stepmom. Some kids have never known their mom. Some moms have passed away, and some have moved away. Every child has some thoughts about his mom.

Isaiah 49:15 says, "Can a woman forget her nursing child, or lack compassion for the child of her womb? Even if these forget, yet I will not forget you." Moms are often described as compassionate. They comfort and nurture their children, no matter how old their children get. This may be a conversation that has not been had before. What does your teen think of his mom? What things does he love about her? What questions does he have?

NOTES:

_____

_____

_____

_____

_____

_____

_____

20. WHAT IS ONE BIG QUESTION YOU HAVE ABOUT GOD?

Have you ever had a question about God but did not have the platform to ask it? You can provide your teen with a place to ask a question she has had about God for a while. Be ready to answer with "I don't know." Your teen will probably ask you a question that you may not know the answer to. You may also get asked a question that no one has the answer to. Both of those scenarios are perfectly okay. The point is to generate conversation and allow your teen to know that asking tough questions is acceptable and invited.

1 Thessalonians 5:11 says, "Therefore encourage one another and build each other up as you are already doing." Paul encourages the church to encourage each other. Encouragement usually comes in the form of conversation. By opening the floor for your teen to ask questions about God, you are opening up a perfect opportunity to encourage her to continue asking questions and seeking God. Even if you do not provide an answer to the question, you can help discover an answer with your teen and reassure her that it is a good thing to ask questions. What big question does she have but has been unable to ask yet?

NOTES:

_____

_____

_____

_____

_____

_____

_____

JUNE

21. WHAT WOULD YOU MOST LIKE TO DO THIS SUMMER?

Summertime means a break from school, cookouts, and celebrating Independence Day in the United States. For students, it means that they have about seven more hours each day that they do not know how to fill. Summer can be a perfect time to take a family vacation across the street, across the state, or across the country. Summer is a season of warmth, swimming pools, and even, at times, boredom.

Proverbs 15:13 says, "A joyful heart makes a face cheerful, but a sad heart produces a broken spirit." Parents have lots of preparations to make for the summer. Your teen may be mature enough to stay home with younger siblings. Are you prepared for the summer months? Is your teen prepared for summer? What is something your teen is looking forward to that will help his heart be joyful and not sad? There are many opportunities for activity, other than watching TV and playing video games all day. Summer is a time to make memories that will last a lifetime—or at least until the next summer.

NOTES:

_____

_____

_____

_____

_____

_____

_____

22. WHAT ARE SOME WAYS YOU WOULD LIKE TO HELP THE POOR AND NEEDY?

The poor and needy are everywhere. Sometimes, it just takes some intentional searching to find them. Helping those in need is one of the most satisfying things you can do on earth. Helping gives you a sense that you are making a difference in the world. It feels wonderful to know that you are helping someone who probably needs and wants your help. You also get to be a blessing to someone else's life. You get to provide a sense of hope for the future because you stepped in to help at the right time. Whether you are serving at a rescue mission or helping someone on a street corner, God honors the act of helping those in need.

Hebrews 13:16 says, "Don't neglect to do what is good and to share, for God is pleased with such sacrifices." God loves when you take some of the resources He has given you and share them with others. By serving on a regular basis, you can help instill a servant's heart into your teen. Many kids would love to serve, but often, they do not know where to go or how to serve. There is a great opportunity to serve somewhere together to help the poor and needy in your community. What are your teen's ideas about serving the poor? How would he like to help the community?

NOTES:

_____

_____

_____

_____

_____

_____

_____

23. WHAT DO YOU THINK ABOUT YOUR DAD?

Just like the question about mothers last month, this one is about Dad. Have you ever asked your teen what she thinks about Dad? Does she think Dad is the greatest? Does she think Dad is too harsh or strict? Is she mad at Dad because he left the family a few years back? What does she really enjoy about Dad? Everyone has a different view of Dad that often goes unsaid. Take the time to ask your teen what her real thoughts are about Dad. Oftentimes, this view will shape her view of men, in general, in the world.

1 Chronicles 29:19 says, "Give my son Solomon a whole heart to keep and to carry out all Your commands, Your decrees, and Your statutes, and to build the temple for which I have made provision." King David prayed for his son Solomon. One of the most important things a dad can do is pray for his children. Prayer is a sign of dedicating your child to God and leaning on Jesus to work in the parenting process. Dad will have one of the most significant and influential roles in a child's life. It is important to know what your teen actually thinks about Dad. There are probably many great qualities and thoughts about Dad. There may also be some hurts from Dad from the past that have not been addressed. What does your teen think?

NOTES:

_____

_____

_____

_____

_____

_____

_____

24. WHAT DO YOU THINK ABOUT BAPTISM?

Baptism is a topic that has been discussed countless times throughout history and even to the present day. There are also many different personal views of baptism regarding its purpose. It can probably be widely agreed that baptism is an important thing for Christians. No matter the method or view, most Christians would say that baptism is something that should be done. Baptism can also be something that does not get talked about or researched at home. It will play a significant part in your teen's life when he goes to tell others about Christianity and baptism. You want him to be prepared and not to base his view simply off of what he has heard or experienced, but on Scripture.

Mark 16:16 says, "Whoever believes and is baptized will be saved, but whoever does not believe will be condemned." Among other verses in the Bible, this one affirms that trust in Jesus and His work on the cross is the key to eternal salvation. By faith alone, one is saved. However, baptism is a very important part of the Christian life, representing a commitment to Christ and newness of life. Baptism is a picture of the inward transformation into an eternal child of God. What is your teen's view of baptism? Is it necessary for salvation? What verses from Scripture lead to that view?

NOTES:

_____

_____

_____

_____

_____

_____

_____

JULY

25. What do you think of the military and veterans?

Current military and veterans deserve a lot of respect. Many of these folks selflessly serve their country with the known potential of losing their lives in the process. The U.S. military is one of the reasons we are able to live in a free country today. Many people have given their lives to defend the United States and the people who live in it. July fourth, Independence Day, is a day to honor U.S. independence and the people who made that independence possible.

John 15:13 says, "No one has greater love than this, that someone would lay down his life for his friends." Laying down your life for another is one of the greatest acts of love. You may have family members or friends who have served. Once we get past the spectacular fireworks displays and tremendous barbecue, what is July fourth all about? Take some time and find out what your teen's view of the military is. It may open up a great conversation about sacrifice, love, and care.

NOTES:

_____

_____

_____

_____

_____

_____

_____

26. WHAT DO YOU THINK PRAYING IS?

Prayer—what is it? Lots of people pray. They pray with different words and in different positions. Some fold hands. Some kneel. Some close their eyes, and some lay on the ground. Some pray to the wind and the sky. Some pray to Mary. Some pray to God. Some pray to make requests, and some pray prayers of thanks. With all of these options on prayer, is there a right or wrong way to pray? Who should you pray to?

Jesus talks about prayer in the New Testament. Matthew 6:9-13 says:

> Therefore, you should pray like this: Our Father in heaven, Your name be honored as holy. Your kingdom come. Your will be done on earth as it is in heaven. Give us today our daily bread. And forgive us our debts, as we also have forgiven our debtors. And do not bring us into temptation, but deliver us from the evil one. [For Yours is the kingdom and the power and the glory forever. Amen.]

Jesus taught His disciples a pattern or model of how to pray, not necessarily the exact words to say. Prayer is a chance to communicate directly with God. What does your teen think of prayer?

NOTES:

_____

_____

_____

_____

_____

_____

_____

27. WHAT IS ONE QUESTION YOU HAVE WANTED TO ASK ME?

Teens have lots of questions about their parents. They just may or may not have thought of them yet. Teens want to know about their parents—where they work, what they enjoy, what they were like as teens, what their parents were like. Your teen probably thinks about all of these questions and more. Oftentimes, schedules are so packed that students do not have time to really think about these questions, let alone find the time to sit down and ask them. They would love to know that their mom was in a jazz band or that their dad's favorite food growing up was liver and onions (hey, there could be one out there).

Allowing your teen to ask you questions about your life may be intimidating because you have no clue what she will ask. 1 Thessalonians 2:8 says, "We cared so much for you that we were pleased to share with you not only the gospel of God but also our own lives, because you had become dear to us." It is a beautiful thing to share the truth of the Gospel and life with another. What better opportunity than to share your life with the children who are in your home? You are opening yourself to being vulnerable to your teen; it will be worth it.

NOTES:

_____

_____

_____

_____

_____

_____

_____

28. WHAT DO YOU THINK OF SHARING THE GOSPEL WITH FRIENDS?

Sharing the Gospel, in general, can be an intimidating feat. If it slightly frightens you, that is probably good news because you will be able to relate to your teen. There are lots of questions that create fear and resistance to sharing the best news in the world with another person. What will they think of me? Will they not like me anymore? Will they think I am dumb? What if I do not have the right answers? What if I mess the words up? All of these questions have probably gone through every Christian's mind at some point. They are normal. However, God will be with us when we try to reach others for Him.

Jesus commands us to go and tell people about Him. Mark 16:15 says, "Then He said to them, 'Go into all the world and preach the gospel to the whole creation.'" Jesus told His disciples to go and preach the Good News about eternal life in Jesus to everyone. Jesus knew it would be daunting. He knew it would be scary at times. He knew that rejection would be involved occasionally. Nonetheless, He told His disciples to share the Gospel message to a world that desperately needed it. Is your teen equipped to share the Gospel with friends?

NOTES:

_____

_____

_____

_____

_____

_____

_____

AUGUST

29. Who is someone you do not get along with?

As a parent, you may already know the answer to this question. If there are siblings, the initial response may be a sibling. If it is the case, find out why, and probe your teen to think about it some more. Is there someone at school? A teacher? Someone on the bus? With whom is there some underlying tension, an uneasiness in the stomach when around that person? Teens often have people they do not get along with but sometimes keep that information to themselves. You may help lower your teen's stress by letting her know she can talk with you about the situation.

People we perceive as enemies can provide a great opportunity to depend on God. Psalm 138:7 says, "If I walk into the thick of danger, You will preserve my life from the anger of my enemies. You will extend Your hand; Your right hand will save me." God is our ultimate Defender when it comes to people we do not get along with. When our identity is secure in Christ, we can walk confidently, knowing that God is over all situations. We should strive to make peace with anyone we have a conflict with. Talking about it may be the first step to resolving the issue. The sooner the conflict is discussed in a healthy way, the sooner it can begin to be resolved. Who is your teen in conflict with?

NOTES:

_____

_____

_____

_____

_____

_____

30. WHAT IS ONE OF YOUR FAVORITE BIBLE STORIES?

Think about this question for yourself first. What is one of *your* favorite Bible stories? Is it Noah and the ark? Is it Jonah and the big fish? Or maybe Jesus walking on water? It is always interesting to hear what people consider their favorite Bible stories. It is even more interesting to hear why. Sometimes, the reason is someone thinks the particular story is just really cool. Other times, the reason is the story somehow connects with the reality of life.

Maybe they have learned Bible stories from you, at church, or from a movie. Wherever the story was learned, it is important to read the biblical account of the story. Psalm 119:105 says, "Your word is a lamp for my feet and a light on my path." The Bible contains true stories that can help us live our lives. There are different characteristics from biblical characters that we can choose to emulate in our own journey of being more like Christ. What is your teen's favorite story?

NOTES:

_____

_____

_____

_____

_____

_____

_____

31. What is your favorite thing to learn about?

Is this a "favorite school subject" question? Not necessarily. More than likely, your teen will resort to thinking about her favorite subject in school because that is a question that is often asked by parents and family. This question expands the range of possibilities to anything in the world. This is more about curiosity. Most people like to learn about something. People like to learn about things like presidents, race cars, trees, and math. Help probe their intellectual curiosity.

Continual learning is one of the markers of successful people. Proverbs 1:5 says, "A wise man will listen and increase his learning, and a discerning man will obtain guidance." Those who are wise listen to others and increase in their knowledge. Desiring to learn and being curious about a particular subject makes it much easier and more fun to learn new information. You may discover something your teen really enjoys learning about when you expand the boundaries outside of school subjects.

NOTES:

_____

_____

_____

_____

_____

_____

_____

32. WHO IS ONE PERSON YOU WANT TO PRAY FOR?

Prayers can easily become solely self-focused prayers in which we pray only for the things that we want. We should pray for things for ourselves. However, we should not pray only for ourselves. We have family and friends, schools and jobs, and political figures that we have knowledge about and can pray for. Maybe there is an elderly woman at church or a single dad or a friend from school who needs prayer.

1 Timothy 2:1 says, "First of all, then, I urge that petitions, prayers, intercessions, and thanksgivings be made for everyone." Praying for others is very important to God. Prayers are not just for Christians, but for everyone. Ask your teen to think of someone who he would like to pray for. It could be a teacher, friend, or family member. It will be interesting to hear who God has put on his heart to pray for. It will also create a unique bonding experience in which you both can pray together for someone specific.

NOTES:

_____

_____

_____

_____

_____

_____

_____

SEPTEMBER

33.   WHAT IS ONE OF YOUR FAVORITE ACTIVITIES?

Everyone has some favorite things they like to do. Activities are things that can easily bond two people. A common, mutual interest is one of the catalysts to good friendships. Do you know what your teen's favorite activities are? Is she really into sports or music? Does she enjoy hunting or drawing? Whatever the activity, finding out what your teen enjoys doing can give you a pathway into making deeper and more meaningful connections.

Doing these activities together can actually be a way to bring glory to God. Colossians 3:17 says, "And whatever you do, in word or in deed, do everything in the name of the Lord Jesus, giving thanks to God the Father through Him." Everything that we do can, in some way, be honoring to God. Showing your teen you love her through a mutual activity can bring glory to God. We can thank God for the enjoyable activities we get to participate in. What are your teen's favorite activities?

NOTES:

_____

_____

_____

_____

_____

_____

_____

34. DO YOU THINK GOD LISTENS TO YOU?

This is a question that a lot of people ask. Does God hear us? Is He hearing us all the time or only when He wants to? Sometimes, it can seem like God must be too busy for us, since other people have much worse problems than we do. It can feel like God does not really hear our prayers when they are not answered in the way we want them to be answered. After a few times, we may not want to even pray anymore. There is hope; God listens.

Psalm 145:18 says, "The Lord is near all who call out to Him, all who call out to Him with integrity." God desires that we call out to Him in prayer. He wants us to want Him. He says that when we have integrity in our Christian walk and life, He is near to us. He promises to always be with us, and He is never too busy for us. While He may listen to our prayers, He will not automatically answer our prayers in the way that we want. His plans are higher and better than ours. He listens to His people. What does your teen think?

NOTES:

_____

_____

_____

_____

_____

_____

_____

35. Outside of family, whom do you trust the most?

Trust, in general, is something that continues to dwindle. The tragedy of 9/11 brought an overarching cloud of distrust in the airline industry. Some news reports about police have grown into a distrust of law enforcement. Law enforcement officers' distrust of civilians has developed from those same reports. Parents often do not let their children play at parks by themselves. Some people do not trust elected officials to do what is in the people's best interest. Some do not even trust God. There are lots of different relationships between people in which trust is not present.

However, there are also many relationships in which trust is high. Proverbs 12:15 says, "A fool's way is right in his own eyes, but whoever listens to counsel is wise." A wise person is one who listens to the godly advice of others. Usually, there is a certain level of trust for a person to ask and receive the godly counsel of another person. One is probably not likely to listen to a person he does not trust. God gives us certain people whom we feel comfortable trusting. Who is one person, outside of your family, that your teen trusts? Is that person trustworthy from your perspective?

NOTES:

_____

_____

_____

_____

_____

_____

_____

36. IS GOD SOMEONE YOU CAN TRUST?

We would probably all say that we can trust God, or at least we want to believe that we can trust God. Sometimes, we have lost trust in God when things are not going our way. We take an illness or death in the family as if God is not in control. When the anger and resentment build against God, we start to not trust Him. Though we can think and feel this way at times, God is trustworthy and is always in control.

Proverbs 3:5 says, "Trust in the Lord with all your heart, and do not rely on your own understanding." God commands us to trust in Him. He is outside of time and is the Creator of the universe. He sent Jesus to be a sacrifice for us. He knows what happens in the end, and He has already won the war against Satan. His thoughts are higher than ours, and His ways higher than ours. While even at times it may seem like situations are out of His hands, they are not. He has full control. Nothing happens without Him allowing it. He can be trusted and has our best interest in mind. Does your teen think God can be trusted?

NOTES:

_____

_____

_____

_____

_____

_____

_____

OCTOBER

37. DO YOU THINK I HAVE EVER BEEN MEAN?

Open the door to vulnerability. No one wants to be mean to their child or even appear mean. The truth is that everyone has been mean at some point in time. This is not to invite a verbal stoning on your character, but rather, to open a conversation that could be very helpful as you continue bringing up your teen. The answer to this question may point out at least two things: times when you have actually been mean, and times when you were only perceived as mean. The conversation from this question will help you understand your teen's perspective even more and provide space for clarification.

Ephesians 6:4 says, "Fathers, don't stir up anger in your children, but bring them up in the training and instruction of the Lord." Discipline and training need to occur in the home. It is God's mandate to parents. However, the demands and requirements on kids should not be unreasonable or impossible. Kids develop physically and mentally at different rates. They cognitively interpret and understand information in different ways as they develop. What is your teen's perspective on "being mean"? How can you use this vulnerable question to understand your teen more?

NOTES:

_____

_____

_____

_____

_____

_____

38. WHAT DO YOU THINK ABOUT CHURCH?

If you do or do not attend church regularly, you probably have a particular view of what church is or what it should be. Your teen probably has a unique perspective on church based on previous experience and the words of others. Does your teen think church is boring, fun, or something else? Does he know what the word "church" means? Is church a building? Is church an event people go to? Is church the people?

1 Corinthians 12:27 says, "Now you are the body of Christ, and individual members of it." The body of Christ is the church. Those who have put their trust in Jesus Christ are the church. Church is also where Christians gather together to worship God, typically on Saturdays or Sundays. What your teen thinks of church will play a big role in what he thinks of God. If he views church as enjoyable and loving, he is more likely to be more drawn to God. A negative view of church can easily lead someone to have less of an interest in pursuing God. Does your teen enjoy his peers in the Sunday school class? Are some of the student ministry events fun for him? What does he think of his church leaders?

NOTES:

_____

_____

_____

_____

_____

_____

_____

39. WHAT DO YOU THINK ABOUT HALLOWEEN?

Halloween is a controversial subject in some Christian and non-Christian homes. October thirty-first is a day when lots of little children dress up in costumes and go trick-or-treating around neighborhoods. They may dress up as scary creatures, like ghosts or vampires, or wear cuter outfits, like pumpkins or bumble bees. They stroll from door to door, hoping for the treat of candy. Some churches have gone the trunk-or-treat route in hopes of providing a safer environment to create a more enjoyable experience. Junior high is about the age where some consider it uncool to continue participating in the trick-or-treat festivities.

Ephesians 5:15 says, "Pay careful attention, then, to how you walk—not as unwise people but as wise." God wants us to be wise people who constantly walk in His light. Halloween in the West is mostly about kids getting candy and parents hiding it later. As far as right or wrong, it is up to you. Is it wise for you? Are you a light for Christ? Your teen is sure to have some thoughts about Halloween that you have not heard yet. What does your teen think about Halloween?

NOTES:

_____

_____

_____

_____

_____

_____

_____

40. WHY DID GOD MAKE PEOPLE?

God made people because . . . (you fill in the blank). Most people have asked this question at some point. It is one of the greatest questions that can be asked. People are such a unique part of creation. We walk, talk, play, create, invent, discover, help, feel, and think. We are much different than the rest of creation—such as rocks, trees, and birds. What is our purpose? Why did God choose to make mankind?

Revelation 4:11 says, "Our Lord and God, You are worthy to receive glory and honor and power, because You have created all things, and because of Your will they exist and were created." God is the Creator of all things, including people. God created us for His glory and honor. He created us to worship Him. He made us to praise Him forever. When we are glorifying God, we are living up to our potential. We are most fulfilled when we are in a right relationship with God. When we worship Him, we experience the most joy we can experience. Why does your teen think God made people?

NOTES:

_____

_____

_____

_____

_____

_____

_____

NOVEMBER

41. WHAT DO YOU THINK ABOUT VOTING?

November is voting time, and voting time means heightened emotions and mixed reviews. Republican or Democrat? Independent or Green? Federal, state, or local? Who is lying the least? Who is lying the most? Are all politicians crooked? And then throw the media into the mix. Where does the information come from? Is it reliable? Is it true or just partially true? A complete lie? Should Christians vote? Will God smite you if you do not vote? There are hundreds of questions when it comes to voting. Your teen will hear lots of people, informed and uninformed, talking about voting and political candidates. Much of the information that circulates comes in bits and pieces of truths and lies from social media and friends. One thing is for sure: God is still in control and on the throne.

Psalm 22:28 says, "For kingship belongs to the Lord; He rules over the nations." God is the ultimate President, Ruler, and King over the universe. No matter what happens, God is still in power over everything and everyone. God's control should be comforting, knowing that, somehow, God will use leaders to bring glory to Himself. With God in ultimate control, Christians should vote for Christian leaders who will honor God first and be public servants. God's wisdom and Spirit is with those who honor Him with their lives. Voting is one way that people can support godly people who are serving the public. What does your teen think of voting?

NOTES:

---

42. WHAT DO YOU THINK OF THE TRINITY?

The term "Trinity" is not specifically mentioned in the Bible but is very real. This is one of the toughest concepts to wrap our minds around. No one can fully and truly comprehend the Trinity. If anyone could, he would fully comprehend God. God the Father, God the Son, and God the Holy Spirit compose the Trinity. This is a significant part of orthodox Christian doctrine. Many different sects are divided over this issue. Your teen is curious. She will want to know how this works. How is God all three Persons, but only one God? It will be a challenge to explain, and she will not fully understand. But have faith and trust that God will make Himself known.

One of the clearest verses where all three Persons of the Godhead are present is Matthew 28:19, which says, "Go, therefore, and make disciples of all nations, baptizing them in the name of the Father and of the Son and of the Holy Spirit." Jesus gives the disciples the command to go and make disciples of all nations. He very clearly acknowledges that God is Father, Son, and Spirit; and all three Persons are the one true God. Some have used a Neapolitan ice cream illustration, which may be close to understanding the Trinity; but it is still a very difficult concept. Each color represents a Person of God, while all of it is still ice cream. However, there are many other verses from Genesis to Revelation that point to the three-Person Godhead. How does your teen view the Trinity?

NOTES:

_____

_____

_____

_____

_____

_____

43. WHAT FOOD WOULD YOU LIKE TO LEARN TO COOK?

Is your teen a food connoisseur? How do you know? Many kids would actually like to experiment with cooking things other than frozen pizza, hot dogs, and Pop-tarts®; they just do not have someone with the time or patience to make some messy creations. Cooking can be a fun task to do together. You can talk while you cook. You can simultaneously show him how the stove works and get dinner ready for the family. Food is one of the things that every human being needs to survive. Why not make it fun and healthy?

1 Corinthians 10:31 says, "Therefore, whether you eat or drink, or whatever you do, do everything for God's glory." You can even have fun cooking and eating for God's glory. God has put so many natural and good foods on the earth for people to enjoy. Help your teen create a new potato dish or a juicy steak. Have some bonding over God's great food. What would your teen like to learn to cook?

NOTES:

_____

_____

_____

_____

_____

_____

_____

44. Did someone make God?

A common question that most people have asked at some point in life is, "Who made God?" Nearly one hundred percent of everything we know in the world was created somehow. Of everything we know to be created, all of it had a Creator. What about God? Did He have a creator? If God did have a creator, then who created God's creator? Then who created the creator who created God? Following this logic, there would be an infinite number of creators and no ultimate Creator. We know this to be impossible. There are many resources and apologists, like William Lane Craig and Frank Turek, to give more specifics and insight to this question.

God has always existed. Psalm 90:2 says, "Before the mountains were born, before You gave birth to the earth and the world, from eternity to eternity, You are God." God existed before the earth and the world. He existed before anything was made. He has always existed and will always exist. He is outside of time and space. He had no beginning and will have no end. That is God. No one created God. What does your teen think about the idea of someone creating God?

NOTES:

_____

_____

_____

_____

_____

_____

_____

DECEMBER

45. WHAT IS YOUR FAVORITE SOCIAL MEDIA APP?

From the wisest in the population to little children in grade school, it seems like nearly everyone has a smartphone these days. Most interact on some type of social media platform. Even if your teen does not have her own account on social media, chances are very good that she still has opinions about which platform is her favorite. Apps continue to be developed on a daily basis, and no one can keep up with them all. Teens are also continually finding ways to engage in social media on platforms that are far away from their parents. This is not meant to be an interrogation question, but rather, one in which you can truly find out what apps your teen enjoys—or would enjoy—and why.

Psalm 127:3 says, "Sons are indeed a heritage from the Lord, children, a reward." God has given children to parents as a reward, a heritage. Parents should treasure their children and bring them up in the training of the Lord. Getting to know your teen will allow you to develop a deeper, more trusting relationship with her. Teens want to know that you care about and love them. They also want you to ask them about more than school and sports practice. From the spiritual to the mundane, teens want to have these various conversations. Even talking about your teen's preference in social media can be a relationship-building bridge. What are your teen's views on social media apps?

NOTES:

_____

_____

_____

_____

_____

_____

_____

46. WHY DO YOU CELEBRATE CHRISTMAS?

Christmas is one of the most celebrated holidays in America. Even some who do not claim to be Christians will celebrate Christmas, or at least attend a church service. Stores have huge displays and promotions just for Christmas. Lots of people decorate the exterior of their homes and put up Christmas trees. Ornaments, candy, cookies, presents, Santa, family, and vacation are all enveloped into Christmas. What is Christmas, and why do you celebrate it?

Jesus is the reason for Christmas. Matthew 1:21 says, "She will give birth to a son, and you are to name Him Jesus, because He will save His people from their sins." The birth of the Savior, Jesus, is the whole reason to celebrate Christmas. Jesus came to the earth in the form of a little human baby to save people from their sins. He was fully God and fully man. He willingly came to earth to be born and die for the sins of the world. Without the birth of Jesus, there is no Christmas. What does your teen think about the reason for Christmas?

NOTES:

_____

_____

_____

_____

_____

_____

_____

47. What non-family member would you like to buy a present for?

Christmas is just around the corner. It may even be too late to be thinking about still buying gifts. In today's world, it is never too late to buy gifts. Most of the time, we think about buying gifts for our family. What about blessing someone outside of your family with a gift? It could even be someone who does not receive Christmas presents. Buying a gift for someone else is a great way to practice generosity around Christmas. It is a satisfying feeling to bless someone who does not expect it.

Proverbs 19:17 says, "Kindness to the poor is a loan to the Lord, and He will give a reward to the lender." Giving is one of the most rewarding parts of life. Giving to those in need and showing kindness is actually the same as giving directly to God. He loves when one person gives generously to another who is in need. He also says He will reward the person who was kind and generous. That reward may be something here on earth, but it is probably a heavenly reward. Who does your teen want to bless this year?

NOTES:

_____

_____

_____

_____

_____

_____

_____

48. HOW WAS JESUS BORN?

It seems like a pretty obvious question. It also seems like an awkward question. How was Jesus born? There are millions of cute (and not-so-cute) nativity scenes in yards and on display tables. Baby Jesus is lying in the manger, all wrapped up. These people in robes are kneeling and are illuminated with bright lightbulbs. How did the baby Jesus get there? You probably know how Jesus came to be born, but does your teen? If she does know, does she believe it?

Isaiah 7:14 says, "Therefore, the Lord Himself will give you a sign: The virgin will conceive, have a son, and name him Immanuel." Jesus, God in the flesh, was born of a virgin girl. This seems unlikely by all accounts, but it is true. The Holy Spirit put Jesus inside of Mary to be born in the most miraculous way. Only God could have made Jesus be born that way. The virgin birth is argued both for and against. However, Scripture is clear that Jesus was born of a virgin. He is a miraculous and powerful God, and nothing is too difficult for Him—even a virgin birth. How does your teen think Jesus was born?

NOTES:

_____

_____

_____

_____

_____

_____

_____

EXTRA WEEKS

49. What is your purpose in life?

Why are you here? Why is anyone here? What is the purpose? Maybe you have already covered the question of why God created people. If so, then you know that God created people to worship Him and bring Him glory. This question is more personal. What is *your* personal purpose? What skills and abilities has God gifted you with? How can you use what God has given you to love God and love people? The answer to these questions will start to move you into the direction of knowing God's purpose for your life. You know the ultimate purpose; now, what does that practically look like for you? Beginning to explore this question for yourself will help you as you navigate this question with your teen.

Isaiah 43:7 says, "Everyone called by My name and created for My glory. I have formed him; indeed, I have made him." God's purpose for His people is to bring Himself glory. The follow-up question is, "How can I obey God to bring Him glory?" Glory to God comes through fear of and obedience to Him. While each person's purpose is to glorify God, it looks different in practice for each person. A large part of obedience to God and loving Him through the teenage years is obeying parents and other authority figures. It can also be glorifying to God for your teen to pray for and help the people he encounters on a daily basis. What does your teen think about his purpose in life?

NOTES:

_____

_____

_____

_____

_____

_____

50.   Is God important in your everyday life?

Is God important in your everyday life? Intuitively, most people would answer this question with yes. That answer would be correct. The depth of the question will probably be especially tough for most teens—and even most people in America. Do we actually need God in our everyday lives? Do we only need God when there is a crisis that we cannot solve? We have grocery stores for food and gas stations for gas. Most people have houses, clothes, running water, and opportunities for education. What is left for God? Is God important in mundane, everyday life?

Proverbs 3:5-6 says, "Trust in the Lord with all your heart, and do not rely on your own understanding; think about Him in all your ways, and He will guide you on the right paths." God wants us to trust Him in everything. He also wants us to remember and think about Him in everything we do. When we acknowledge Him in all our ways, He promises to guide us in the way we should go. Many times, we do not think about God unless something tragic happens, or we are asking for something. How can God be important in every aspect of everyday?

NOTES:

_____

_____

_____

_____

_____

_____

51. If you could change one thing in life, what would it be?

Most people want to be better at something or wish something would be different in some way. Oftentimes, the answer to this question will drive a person to have a tremendous impact on humanity. Think about inventions. Most inventions were created because someone wanted something to be different in the world. Henry Ford wanted more people to have cars. George Washington Carver wanted people to use natural resources for more everyday uses. Change can be for better or for worse. Mainly think of change for the better, for improvement. Improvement and betterment of people and things can provide help for humanity and even draw people to God.

Galatians 2:20 says, "And I no longer live, but Christ lives in me. The life I now live in the body, I live by faith in the Son of God, who loved me and gave Himself for me." God gave His life so that we could become new people. "Changed people" is a common theme and goal of the Bible. When we have God, He continually changes us to be more like Him. No one is perfect. If we are not changing to become godlier, we are not developing in godliness as God intends. Out of our gratitude and love for God, we should always be open to allowing Him to change our hearts, which will then change our actions. When we change, we influence change in others as well. What is something your teen would like to change?

NOTES:

_____

_____

_____

_____

_____

_____

_____

52. What would life be like with no God?

Think about life with no God. This can be an interesting trip into imagining a life with no God. If you are a Christian, chances are that even reading the question by itself brought a type of gloom to your mind. What if there were no ultimate Creator Who governed the universe? Where would morals come from? How would people decide what is right and wrong? What reason would there be for life? Would there even be life? Who would be the example of love? Would people even know what love is? What if there were no rules in life? What if there were no eternal safe haven in heaven? This question will help your teen see the enormous benefit of God being real and present.

Isaiah 41:10 says, "Do not fear, for I am with you; do not be afraid, for I am your God. I will strengthen you; I will help you; I will hold on to you with My righteous right hand." God tells us that He is always with us. He tells us not to be afraid. Who would not want Someone in Whom they can find eternal comfort? Who would not want someone to forever strengthen them? Who would not want someone to eternally help them? Who would not want the Creator of the universe as a Protector? Without God, none of those things are possible. With God, they all are possible! Life without God would be devastating and hopeless. What does your teen think life would be like with no God?

NOTES:

_____

_____

_____

_____

_____

_____

_____

I pray you have found this book helpful in connecting with your teenager. The parenting years can be difficult, busy, and strenuous, but your kids are worth it. Teaching them God's ways is worth it. Modeling godliness is worth it. Taking extra time to have face-to-face conversations is worth it. May God give you the strength, endurance, and energy to keep parenting well.

THE END

For more information about
Derek Rowe
&
52 Conversations to Have with Your Teen

please visit:

www.derektrowe.com
@derektrowe

For speaking engagements, please email Derek at derek@derektrowe.com.

For more information about
AMBASSADOR INTERNATIONAL
please visit:

www.ambassador-international.com
@AmbassadorIntl
www.facebook.com/AmbassadorIntl

If you enjoyed this book, please consider leaving us a review on
Amazon, Goodreads, or our website.

www.ingramcontent.com/pod-product-compliance
Lightning Source LLC
Chambersburg PA
CBHW072044040426
42447CB00012BB/3016